COOKING FOR ONE

Edited by
Valerie Creek

Contents

This edition first published 1979 by
Octopus Books Limited
59 Grosvenor Street, London W.1.

© 1979 Octopus Books Limited

ISBN 0 7064 1013 0

Produced and printed in Hong Kong by
Mandarin Publishers Limited
22a Westlands Road, Quarry Bay

Frontispiece: SWEET AND SOUR AVOCADO *(page 19)*
(Photograph: Carmel Produce Information Bureau)

Weights and Measures

All measurements in this book are based on Imperial weights and measures, with American equivalents given in parenthesis.

Measurements in *weight* in the Imperial and American system are the same. Liquid measurements are different, and the following table shows the equivalents:

Liquid measurements

1 Imperial pint	20 fluid ounces
1 American pint	16 fluid ounces
1 American cup	8 fluid ounces

Level spoon measurements are used in all the recipes.

Spoon measurements

1 tablespoon (1T)	15 ml
1 teaspoon	5 ml

INTRODUCTION

This is no ordinary cookbook; it has been specially designed for the many people of all ages and from every walk of life who cater for themselves. Many busy cooks with the fads and fancies of a family to consider may look with envy at those with only themselves to please. It is true that many single people take great pleasure in preparing and cooking favourite dishes, but there are others who find it a chore for which it is difficult to summon the energy or enthusiasm. A glance at the delicious selection of recipes in 'Cooking for One' may well serve to tempt a waning appetite and raise flagging spirits. It really is not necessary to be an expert cook to eat well; not one of the dishes included here requires special culinary skills or hours of preparation time.

Every single person needs wholesome, balanced meals to keep fit and well. Unfortunately, people living alone too often take the easy way out and buy canned, packaged and pre-cooked foods which need the minimum of preparation. The 'right' foods often seem dull and unexciting. The chapter on interesting ways with vegetables and salads can help here, with such tempting ideas as Breda Stuffed Cabbage and Crunchy Leek Bake. Breakfast, too, is an essential ingredient to good health and yet it is the one meal that many people go without. We have therefore included some nourishing drinks in the breakfast chapter which are quick and simple to prepare, and which contain enough food value to provide the energy necessary to last the morning.

With the problem of a balanced diet solved, there are still the difficulties of keeping within a careful budget. Anyone who has lived alone knows the problems and pitfalls of shopping for fresh produce in usable quantities, and has faced the difficulties of using up those extra, unnecessary ingredients. There are really no easy solutions, but a few hints may help. For example, do try to buy fruit and vegetables from market stalls where you are not confined to pre-weighed and packaged foods. If you own a small freezer it is an excellent idea to make up several dishes and freeze complete meals for future use. Finally, pay special attention to storage and invest in cling film (plastic wrap) and foil as well as good airtight containers, to keep those unused ingredients fresh.

'Cooking for One' has been designed to encourage single people to make meals more interesting and to devote a little extra time to preplanning. Planning, after all, is essential for successful entertaining. Many of these dishes can be prepared using double quantities, to produce the perfect dinner party menu.

CRUMBED LAMB CHOP *(page 34)*

BREAKFAST DISHES

Kipper Kedgeree

1 oz. (2 T) long-grain rice
4 tablespoons (¼ cup) stock
2 kipper fillets, roughly chopped
½ oz. (1 T) butter, melted

1 hard-boiled egg, chopped
little chopped parsley
pinch of cayenne pepper

This is an old traditional breakfast dish. Put the rice and stock in a saucepan, together with the kippers. Bring to the boil and stir once, then cover the pan and simmer for 15 minutes, or until the rice is tender and has absorbed the liquid. Add the butter, hard-boiled egg and parsley. Spoon onto a warmed serving plate and sprinkle the cayenne pepper over the top.

Sunshine Breakfast

½ grapefruit
1 tablespoon raisins

1 tablespoon sultanas (seedless
white raisins)

Carefully remove the flesh from the grapefruit, reserving the shell. Chop the flesh roughly, then mix with the raisins and sultanas (white raisins). Pile the mixture back into the shell and serve chilled.
Note: Keep the remaining ½ grapefruit, cut side down on a saucer, in the refrigerator for use at another meal (for example, Crab and Grapefruit Cocktail on page 18).

Muesli

1 oz. (¾ cup) rolled oats
  (oatmeal)
1 tablespoon sultanas (seedless
  white raisins)
1 tablespoon raisins

½ oz. (2 T) chopped mixed nuts
1 tablespoon soft brown sugar
¼ pint (⅔ cup) plain yogurt
1 eating apple, cored and chopped

Combine the oats, dried fruit, nuts and sugar. Pour on the yogurt
and mix to a creamy consistency. Spoon into a cereal bowl and top
with the chopped apple. Serve chilled.

Muesli may be mixed at night, covered and kept in the
refrigerator, ready to serve for breakfast the following morning.

Bacon Raisin Toast

2 streaky bacon rashers (slices)
1 tablespoon raisins

1 slice of bread
butter

Grill (broil) the bacon until crisp. Roughly chop it and mix with the
raisins. Toast the bread on both sides and butter liberally. Top the
toast with the bacon and raisin mixture. Serve hot.

Peptail

1 egg
½ pint (1 ¼ cups) chilled orange
juice

This makes a quick, yet nourishing breakfast when you are in a hurry. Whisk the egg well, then add the orange juice. Strain into a large glass and drink immediately.

Pineapple or grapefruit juice may be used instead of orange, if preferred.

Iced Minted Tea

½ oz. (1 T) tea leaves
½ pint (1 ¼ cups) cold water
1 orange, sliced

ice cubes
few leaves of fresh mint

A refreshing drink for a quick breakfast. Place the tea in a jug and pour over the cold water. Leave overnight to infuse. The next morning, strain into a large glass and add the orange slices and ice cubes. Top with mint leaves. Serve cold.

Tea Nog

1 cup freshly made tea
1 egg
1 tablespoon honey

Another quick breakfast idea. Pour the tea into a mug. Whisk in the egg and honey with a fork and drink while still hot.

PEPTAIL
(Photograph: British Egg Information Service)

SOUPS AND APPETIZERS

Sausage and Onion Soup

1 onion, sliced
½ oz. (1 T) butter
1 teaspoon gravy powder
6 fl. oz. (¾ cup) water
½ garlic clove, crushed
little made mustard

salt and pepper
1 pork and beef sausage, cut into
 chunks
1 oz. (¼ cup) Cheddar cheese,
 grated

Fry the onion in the butter for about 5 minutes. Mix the gravy
powder with a little water then stir into the remaining water and add
to the onion with the garlic, mustard, salt and pepper. Simmer for 30
minutes.

Add the sausage and simmer for a further 10 minutes. Pour into a
warmed soup bowl and sprinkle the grated cheese on top. Serve hot.

14

Spinach Soup

½ oz. (1 T) butter or margarine
½ oz. (2 T) flour
¼ pint (⅔ cup) milk
1 teaspoon grated onion
¼ pint (⅔ cup) chicken stock

8 oz. (1 cup) frozen creamed
  spinach
salt and pepper
pinch of grated nutmeg
1 tablespoon double (heavy) cream

Melt the butter or margarine in a saucepan and stir in the flour. Cook for 1 minute, then stir in the milk, onion and chicken stock. Bring to the boil. Add the spinach, salt, pepper and grated nutmeg. Cook for a further 5 minutes. Pour into a warmed soup bowl and swirl the cream over the surface just before serving. Serve hot.
Note: Use only a small piece of a stock (bouillon) cube, when making the chicken stock.

Bacon and Cheese Soup

1 streaky bacon rasher (slice),
  chopped
½ onion, chopped
1 oz. (¼ cup) flour
4 tablespoons (¼ cup) chicken stock
4 tablespoons (¼ cup) milk

½ carrot, thinly sliced
salt and pepper
1 oz. (¼ cup) Cheddar cheese,
  grated
chopped parsley to garnish

Fry the bacon in its own fat for 3 minutes. Add the onion and cook for a further 3 minutes. Stir in the flour, then gradually stir in the stock and milk. Bring to the boil. Add the carrot, salt and pepper and simmer for 20 minutes. Remove from the heat and stir in the cheese. Pour into a warmed soup bowl and sprinkle the chopped parsley over the top. Serve hot.

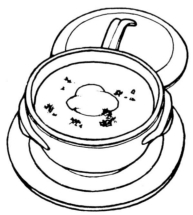

Spanish Vegetable Soup

2 leaves of green cabbage, shredded
1 tomato, sliced
1/4 green pepper, cored, seeded and
  sliced
1/2 onion, sliced

1/2 garlic clove, crushed
1/4 pint (2/3 cup) chicken stock
salt and pepper
1 oz. (2 slices) smoked sausage,
  chopped

Put the cabbage, tomato, green pepper, onion, garlic, stock, salt and
pepper into a saucepan. Bring to the boil, then simmer for 40
minutes. Add the smoked sausage and reheat gently. Pour into a
warmed soup bowl and serve hot.

Note: Leftover vegetables, such as green peppers and onions, can be
wrapped in cling film (plastic wrap) and kept for use at another meal
(for example, Spanish Omelette page 23).

Smoked Fish Pâté

1 large kipper fillet
2 oz. (1/4 cup) butter
pepper
few drops of lemon juice
hot buttered toast

Garnish:
sprig of parsley
slice of lemon

Remove the skin and bones from the kipper fillet. Put the flesh in a
bowl with the butter and pepper to taste and mash well together
until a smooth paste is formed. Stir in the lemon juice, then spoon
into a small dish. Chill in the refrigerator for at least 20 minutes.
Garnish with parsley and a slice of lemon. Serve with hot buttered
toast.

Note: Wrap any remaining cut lemon in cling film (plastic wrap)
and keep in the refrigerator for use with fish or to sprinkle over
sliced apple, avocado or banana to prevent discoloration.

SMOKED FISH PÂTÉ
(Photograph: Dairy Produce Advisory Service M.M.B.)

Crab and Grapefruit Cocktail

2 oz. (¼ cup) canned or fresh crab
  meat
1½ tablespoons thick mayonnaise
lettuce leaves

Garnish:
paprika
½ grapefruit, peeled and cut into
  segments

Flake the crab meat and combine with the mayonnaise. Arrange
leaves of lettuce to form a bed on a small plate. Spoon the crab meat
mixture into the centre. Sprinkle paprika over the top and garnish
with the segments of grapefruit.

Corn and Cucumber Cocktail

3 oz. (½ cup) sweetcorn kernels
salt and pepper
pinch of dry mustard
1 tablespoon oil

2 teaspoons malt vinegar
1 hard-boiled egg, chopped
2 inch piece of cucumber, diced
few lettuce leaves

Cook the sweetcorn if frozen, or drain if canned. Beat together the
salt, pepper, mustard, oil and vinegar, then fold in the chopped egg,
cucumber and cooled sweetcorn. Arrange the lettuce leaves on a
small plate to form a bed, then pile the sweetcorn mixture on top.
Serve chilled.

Sweet and Sour Avocado

½ avocado
1 teaspoon caster sugar
1 teaspoon thick mayonnaise
½ eating apple, peeled, cored and
 grated

1 oz. (1 slice) cooked ham,
 chopped
4 oz. (¾ cup) canned sweetcorn
 kernels, drained
sprig of fresh mint to garnish

Remove the avocado stone (pit). Scoop out the flesh and place in a bowl. Add the sugar and mayonnaise and whip together with a fork. Stir in the apple and ham and most of the sweetcorn. Spoon the mixture into the avocado shell and place a rim of sweetcorn around the edge. Top with a sprig of fresh mint and serve immediately.
Note: The remaining ½ avocado will keep if brushed on the cut side immediately with lemon juice and then tightly wrapped in cling film (plastic wrap).

Stuffed Peaches

1 tablespoon sultanas (seedless
 white raisins)
2 oz. (¼ cup) cream cheese
1 tablespoon chopped walnuts

2 canned peach halves
2 small lettuce leaves
sprigs of watercress to garnish

Soak the sultanas (white raisins) in boiling water, then drain and cool.
   Mix the cheese, sultanas (white raisins) and nuts together. Chill in the refrigerator for a few minutes to firm. Arrange the peach halves on the lettuce leaves and fill the centres with the cheese mixture. Garnish with watercress before serving.

Cheese, Melon and Prawn Cocktail

1 slice of honeydew melon
few lettuce leaves, shredded
2 oz. (¼ cup) Cheddar cheese,
  cubed
2 oz. (¼ cup) shelled prawns
  (shrimp)

1 ½ tablespoons thick mayonnaise
1 tablespoon single (light) cream
1 tablespoon tomato ketchup

Remove the seeds from the melon slice, then cut the flesh into small cubes. Place the shredded lettuce in the bottom of a tall wine glass. Pile the melon, cheese and prawns (shrimp) on top. Mix together the mayonnaise, cream and ketchup and pour this sauce over the top. Serve chilled.
Note: Most supermarkets sell slices of melon, but if not, the remaining fruit from a whole melon will keep for 1 to 2 days in the refrigerator if placed in a plastic container, or wrapped in cling film (plastic wrap).

Cod and Tomato Surprise

1 cod fillet
½ oz. (2 T) flour
salt and pepper
½ oz. (1 T) butter

½ small onion, finely chopped
2 teaspoons tomato ketchup
2 tablespoons double (heavy) cream

Coat the cod fillet in flour mixed with salt and pepper, then place in a well-greased small ovenproof dish. Melt the butter in a saucepan and fry the onion until tender. Add the tomato ketchup and cream, stir well together and pour over the fish. Bake in moderate oven, 350°F, Gas Mark 4 for 35 minutes. Serve hot.
Note: Wrap the remaining ½ onion in cling film (plastic wrap) to keep for use in another savoury dish the next day.

CHEESE, MELON AND PRAWN COCKTAIL
(Photograph: Dairy Produce Advisory Service M.M.B.)

Stuffed Aubergine (Eggplant)

1 small aubergine (eggplant)
salt
1 tablespoon oil
1 oz. (1 slice) cooked tongue,
  chopped
onion salt
1 oz. (¼ cup) mushrooms, chopped
small piece of celery, chopped

little chopped parsley
¼ teaspoon dried oregano or mixed
  herbs
beaten egg
1 tablespoon dry breadcrumbs
little grated lemon rind
½ oz. (1 T) margarine

Wipe the aubergine (eggplant) and cut in half lengthways. Using a small sharp knife, make criss-cross cuts in the cut surfaces. Sprinkle with salt and leave, cut sides down, for 30 minutes. Rinse and dry the aubergine (eggplant). Fry in the oil, cut sides down, for about 5 minutes or until the flesh is tender. Remove the flesh, keeping the skin intact, and chop it. Put into a bowl. Place the shells in an ovenproof shallow dish.

Add the tongue, onion salt, mushrooms, celery, parsley and oregano or mixed herbs to the aubergine (eggplant) flesh and mix thoroughly together. Bind with a little beaten egg. Fill each shell with this mixture. Sprinkle the tops with the breadcrumbs and lemon rind and dot with the margarine. Bake in a moderately hot oven, 375°F, Gas Mark 5 for 30-40 minutes. Serve hot.

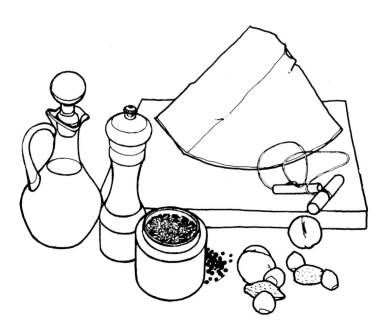

Devilled Sausages on Toast

½ oz. (1 T) butter
2 skinless (link) sausages, sliced
1 streaky bacon rasher (slice),
 chopped
½ small onion, finely sliced
1 tomato, skinned and quartered
pinch of curry powder

½ teaspoon prepared English
 mustard
1 teaspoon tomato ketchup
1 teaspoon chutney
pinch of cayenne pepper
salt and pepper
1 slice of hot buttered toast

Melt the butter in a pan, add the sausages, bacon and onion and fry gently for 5 minutes until lightly coloured. Add the remaining ingredients and cook for a further 5 minutes, stirring constantly.

Pile the mixture onto the hot toast and serve.

Spanish Omelette

½ oz. (1 T) butter
½ onion, finely sliced
½ small green pepper, cored, seeded
 and finely sliced
1 medium-sized potato, boiled and
 sliced

2 eggs
1 tablespoon water
salt and pepper

Melt the butter in a pan, add the onion and pepper and fry gently for 7 minutes until soft. Add the potato and heat through.

Put the eggs in a bowl with the water and seasoning. Beat well to mix, then pour into the pan. Cook gently until the eggs are set, stirring occasionally.

This makes a substantial appetizer and is good served hot or cold.

MAIN COURSES

Fried Plaice (Flounder) Fillet

1 plaice (flounder) fillet
½ tablespoon flour
salt and pepper
beaten egg
dry breadcrumbs
lard for frying

1 large potato, peeled, cut into
  sticks and parboiled
Garnish:
parsley sprigs
lemon slices

Coat the fish in the flour seasoned with a little salt and pepper. Mix together beaten egg with a little water and dip the fillet into this. Coat with breadcrumbs, pressing them on firmly.

Heat lard in a frying pan (skillet) and fry the fish on both sides until light brown and thoroughly cooked. Meanwhile, heat lard in another pan and fry the potatoes for about 5 minutes, or until crisp and golden. Remove from the pan very carefully and drain on paper towels. Garnish the fish with parsley and lemon and serve with the chips (French fries).

FRIED PLAICE (FLOUNDER) FILLET
(Photograph: Danish Food Centre, London)

Mixed Fish Stew

½ oz. (1 T) butter
1 small onion, sliced
1 small leek, chopped
1 celery stalk, chopped
2 tomatoes, quartered
½ garlic clove, crushed
pinch of chopped parsley
few drops of lemon juice

½ small bay leaf
pinch of dried thyme
salt and pepper
6 oz. (1 cup) mixed fish, e.g.
  cod, herring, whiting and
  whitefish, skinned and boned if
  necessary and cut into chunks

Melt the butter in a large saucepan and lightly fry the onion, leek and celery until tender. Stir in the tomatoes, garlic, parsley, lemon juice, bay leaf, thyme, salt and pepper. Add the fish with sufficient water to cover. Bring to the boil, then reduce the heat and simmer for 10 minutes. Serve hot, with mashed potatoes.
Note: Use bottled lemon juice where a recipe requires such a small amount.

Poached Whiting

1 small whiting, cleaned, or 1 cod
  steak
salt and pepper
1 teaspoon lemon juice

1 or 2 leeks, sliced
¼ pint (⅔ cup) water
few mushrooms, sliced
pinch of dried mixed herbs

Sprinkle the fish with salt and pepper and place in a shallow pan with the lemon juice, leeks, water and mushrooms. Cover and simmer gently for 10-12 minutes, basting occasionally. Turn the fish over once during cooking. Add the herbs and serve hot.

Mackerel with Mandarin Sauce

1 mackerel, cleaned
few drops of lemon juice
1 oz. (2 T) butter
salt and pepper
½ small onion, chopped

½ oz. (2 T) flour
3 oz. (½ cup) canned mandarin
  oranges
2 teaspoons white wine vinegar
1 oz. (¼ cup) Edam cheese, grated

Put the fish in a large ovenproof dish. Sprinkle with lemon juice, half
the butter, cut into small pieces, and salt and pepper. Cover and bake
in a moderately hot oven, 375°F, Gas Mark 5 for 20 minutes.

    Meanwhile, cook the onion in the remaining butter in a saucepan
until soft and transparent. Add the flour, salt and pepper and cook
for 1 minute. Drain the mandarin oranges and make up the syrup to
¼ pint (⅔ cup) with the wine vinegar and lemon juice. Gradually stir
this into the pan. Add the cheese and mandarin oranges. Heat
through for 1 minute. Pour the sauce over the fish and serve with
vegetables in season.

Tomato Crumbed Fish

1 cod or haddock fillet
1 tablespoon tomato ketchup
browned breadcrumbs

beaten egg
oil for frying
lemon slices to garnish

Wipe the fish, then spread all over with the tomato ketchup. Coat with browned breadcrumbs, pressing them firmly onto the fish. Dip the fish in beaten egg, then coat again in crumbs. Shallow fry in hot oil for 8-10 minutes, turning once. Drain, then serve hot with croquette potatoes and peas. Serve garnished with lemon slices.

Swiss Cheese Casserole

1 small leek, sliced
1 small onion, sliced
1 small carrot, chopped
1 celery stalk, chopped

2 oz. (½ cup) Cheddar cheese,
 grated
salt and pepper
¼ pint (⅔ cup) milk

Layer the prepared vegetables in a small casserole and sprinkle on most of the cheese. Season with salt and pepper. Pour the milk over the vegetables and cover with a lid. Bake in a moderate oven, 350°F, Gas Mark 4 for 45 minutes.

Remove the casserole from the oven. Stir the vegetables, then sprinkle the remaining cheese over the surface. Return to the oven, uncovered, and bake for a further 15 minutes.

TOMATO CRUMBED FISH, PRAWN (SHRIMP), RICE AND TOMATO SALAD *(page 60)*, SAUCY STEAK *(page 32)*, CHICKEN WITH BARBECUE TOPPING *(page 44)*
(Photograph: Hammonds Sauces)

Beef Crumble

4 oz. (½ cup) minced (ground)
  beef
onion salt
1 teaspoon oil
1 teaspoon gravy powder
¼ pint (⅔ cup) water
4 tablespoons (¼ cup) dry sage and
  onion stuffing

½ oz. (2 T) flour
1 oz. (2 T) butter
1 oz. (¼ cup) Cheddar cheese,
  grated
salt and pepper

Sprinkle the beef with onion salt and fry in the oil until lightly
browned. Dissolve the gravy powder in a little of the water, then add
to the rest. Add this to the meat and stir over a gentle heat until
thickened. Remove from the heat. Put the stuffing mix and flour in a
bowl. Add the butter and rub in until the mixture resembles
breadcrumbs. Add the cheese, salt and pepper and mix thoroughly.

   Put the meat mixture in a small ovenproof dish and sprinkle the
crumble over the surface. Bake in a moderately hot oven, 375°F, Gas
Mark 5 for 40 minutes. Serve hot with green vegetables.

Spaghetti Bolognese

½ small onion, chopped
garlic salt
½ green pepper, cored, seeded and
  diced
oil for frying
4 oz. (½ cup) minced (ground)
  beef
2 canned tomatoes plus 2
  tablespoons can juice

1 tablespoon red wine
2 teaspoons tomato purée (paste)
pinch of dried oregano
salt and pepper
2 oz. (25-50 strands) spaghetti
½ oz. (1 T) butter
1 tablespoon grated Parmesan
  cheese

Fry the onion, garlic salt and green pepper in the oil until tender. Stir
in the meat and brown on all sides. Stir in the tomatoes and can juice,
red wine, tomato purée (paste), oregano, salt and pepper. Simmer
gently for about 30 minutes.

Meanwhile, cook the spaghetti in boiling salted water until tender.
Drain and toss in the butter. Put the spaghetti around the edge of a
warmed shallow dish and pour the meat sauce into the centre.
Sprinkle Parmesan cheese over the surface and serve hot.

Beef Kebab with Rice

4 oz. rump (boneless sirloin) steak,
  ½ inch thick, cut into 1 inch cubes
1 firm tomato, halved
2 small onions, parboiled
2 button mushrooms

2 thick cucumber slices
2 bacon rolls, made from streaky
  bacon rashers (slices)
oil
freshly boiled rice

Thread the steak cubes, tomato, onions, mushrooms, cucumber and
bacon rolls onto a long skewer. Brush with a little oil to prevent the
ingredients from burning. Grill (broil) until tender and golden
brown, turning the skewer frequently. Serve the kebab hot on a bed
of rice.

Saucy Steak

1 rump (boneless sirloin), fillet or
  quick-fry steak

1 tablespoon bottled brown sauce
salt and pepper

Flatten the steak if thick, then spread one side with half of the brown sauce. Lightly season with salt and pepper and grill (broil) for 2-3 minutes, according to taste. Turn the steak over, spread with the remaining sauce and grill (broil) for a further 2-3 minutes. Serve hot, with grilled (broiled) tomatoes and any other vegetables of your choice.

Lamb and Apricot Stew

6 oz. (¾ cup) lean boneless lamb,
  cubed
flour
salt and pepper
½ onion, chopped
1 tablespoon oil

¼ pint (⅔ cup) chicken stock
pinch of dried mixed herbs
1½ oz. (¼ cup) dried apricots,
  soaked overnight and drained
few split blanched almonds

Coat the cubed meat with flour mixed with salt and pepper. Fry the onion in the oil in a saucepan for 3 minutes. Add the lamb cubes and brown on all sides. Stir in the stock then the mixed herbs. Bring to the boil and simmer gently for 1 hour.

    Add the apricots and cook for a further 30 minutes. Scatter almonds over the surface and serve hot.

LAMB AND APRICOT STEW
(Photograph: Pointerware (U.K.) Limited)

Lamb and Lentil Casserole

6 oz. boneless scrag end of neck
  (neck slices) of lamb, diced
1 small onion, chopped
½ small swede (rutabaga) or
  turnip, chopped
¾ pint (2 cups) stock, made with
  yeast (meat) extract

2-3 teaspoons tomato ketchup
salt and pepper
2 oz. (¼ cup) lentils, soaked
  overnight and drained

Brown the lamb in its own fat in a saucepan. Add the onion, swede (rutabaga) or turnip, stock, tomato ketchup, salt and pepper. Cover and simmer gently for about 1 hour. When the meat is just tender, add the lentils and continue to simmer until they are cooked. Serve hot, with potatoes if liked.

Crumbed Lamb Chop

1 lamb chop
salt and pepper
pinch of dried rosemary
flour
beaten egg
browned breadcrumbs

1 oz. (2 T) butter
2 teaspoons oil
3-4 mushrooms
1 tomato
watercress to garnish

Remove any surplus fat from the chop. Mix together the salt, pepper, rosemary and a little flour. Coat the chop in this. Dip in beaten egg, then coat in browned breadcrumbs, pressing them firmly onto the chop. Heat together the butter and oil in a frying pan (skillet). Fry the chop quickly at first, then reduce the heat so that it is cooked for about 5 minutes on each side. Drain and keep hot.

   Fry the mushrooms gently in the remaining fat in the pan for about 2 minutes. Score the top of the tomato and lightly fry for about 4 minutes. Serve the chop and vegetables on a warmed plate, garnished with watercress. Serve immediately.

Veal Roll

1 veal escalope (scallop)
1½ oz. (3 T) butter, softened
½ tablespoon chopped parsley
pinch of dried thyme
few drops of lemon juice

½ oz. (2 T) flour
¼ pint (⅔ cup) chicken stock
salt and pepper
2 tablespoons single (light) cream

Beat the veal escalope (scallop) until very thin. Put half the butter in a bowl and beat in the parsley, thyme and lemon juice. Spread this over the veal. Roll up the veal and secure with string or a wooden cocktail stick. Melt the remaining butter in a frying pan (skillet) and brown the veal on all sides. Remove and keep warm.

Add the flour to the pan and cook for 1 minute. Gradually stir in the stock and bring to the boil, stirring constantly. Season with salt and pepper, replace the veal roll and cover the pan. Simmer gently for about 20 minutes or until the veal is cooked. Remove the veal and place on a warm serving dish. Add the cream to the sauce and heat through gently. Pour this sauce over the veal roll and serve hot, with vegetables in season.

Veal French Style

1 veal escalope (scallop)
flour
beaten egg
1 oz. (2 T) butter

1 tablespoon oil
2 oz. (½ cup) mushrooms, sliced
1 tomato, sliced

Beat the veal until fairly thin. Coat with a little flour, then dip in beaten egg. Heat together the butter and oil in a frying pan (skillet). Fry the veal gently for about 5 minutes on each side, lowering the heat so that the veal is thoroughly cooked. Drain and keep hot.

Fry the mushrooms in the remaining fat in the pan for about 4 minutes until tender. Serve the veal with tomato slices, mushrooms and a green vegetable, such as green beans.

Sausages in Curry Sauce

2 pork sausages
oil for frying
½ small onion, chopped
2 teaspoons curry powder
1 teaspoon gravy powder
¼ pint (⅔ cup) water

½ oz. (1½ T) sultanas (seedless white raisins)
1 teaspoon chutney
½ teaspoon tomato purée (paste)
freshly cooked rice

Fry the sausages in the oil in a frying pan (skillet) for about 15 minutes, turning frequently. Remove the sausages. Lightly fry the onion in the pan for 3-4 minutes until tender. Add the curry powder and cook for a further 2-3 minutes. Mix the gravy powder with a little of the cold water and add to the pan with the sultanas (raisins), chutney, tomato purée (paste) and remaining water.

Cut the sausages into thick wedges and return to the curry sauce. Bring to the boil and simmer for about 15 minutes. Serve the curried sausages on a hot plate surrounded by rice.

Farmer's Sausagemeat Hotpot

4 oz. (½ cup) pork sausagemeat
pinch of dried mixed herbs
1 streaky bacon rasher (slice),
  chopped
1 tomato, sliced
salt and pepper

1 small cooking apple, peeled, cored
  and sliced
1 oz. (¼ cup) Cheddar cheese,
  grated
6 oz. (⅔ cup) mashed potatoes
chopped parsley to garnish

Line the bottom of a small ovenproof dish with the sausagemeat. Sprinkle with the mixed herbs. Gently fry the bacon in its own fat and place in the prepared dish. Add the tomato slices, salt, pepper and apple slices. Sprinkle with the grated cheese. Top with the potatoes. Bake in a moderate oven, 350°F, Gas Mark 4 for 1 hour, or until cooked and golden brown on top. Serve hot, garnished with chopped parsley.

Pork and Pâté Parcel

1 pork loin chop
puff pastry made with 4 oz.
  (1 cup) flour

1 tablespoon pork liver pâté
salt and pepper
beaten egg

Grill (broil) the chop for 5 minutes on each side. Cool. Roll out the dough to a rectangle about 6 × 8 inches. Spread the chop on both sides with the pâté and season, then wrap in the dough, leaving the bone protruding. Seal the edges with beaten egg. Bake in a moderately hot oven, 375°F, Gas Mark 5 for 30 minutes. Serve hot with vegetables in season.

Orange Pork Meatballs

4 oz. (½ cup) minced (ground)
  pork
½ apple, cored and grated
grated rind of ½ orange
4 tablespoons (¼ cup) dry sage and
  onion stuffing mix

beaten egg
1 tablespoon oil
few canned mandarin oranges
1 teaspoon gravy powder
2 teaspoons marmalade

Mix together the pork, apple and half of the orange rind. Make up the stuffing mix according to the directions on the pack, then add to the pork mixture. Bind together with a little beaten egg. Form into 2 or 3 meatballs and chill in the refrigerator for 30 minutes to become firm.

Fry the meatballs gently in the oil until browned on all sides. Place in an ovenproof dish. Drain the mandarin oranges and use a little of the can syrup with water to make ¼ pint (⅔ cup). Mix the gravy powder with a little of this liquid, then stir into the remainder with the marmalade. Pour over the meatballs and cover the dish. Bake in a moderate oven, 350°F, Gas Mark 4 for 45 minutes.

Add the mandarin oranges and return to the oven for a further 15 minutes. Garnish with the remaining orange rind and serve hot with a green vegetable.

Note: Use the remaining fruits from this recipe to make a delicious fruit salad to serve as a dessert to follow. Beaten egg may be used for scrambled eggs or added to mashed potatoes.

Sweet and Sour Pork Slices

3-4 thin slices belly pork (fresh
  pork sides)
¾ tablespoon cornflour (cornstarch)
2 tablespoons cider (hard cider)
2 teaspoons brown sugar

2 teaspoons redcurrant jelly
1 teaspoon soy sauce
2 teaspoons vinegar
1 oz. (½ cup) hot cooked noodles

Grill (broil) the pork slices for 10 minutes on each side. Meanwhile,
mix together the cornflour (cornstarch) and cider, in a saucepan. Add
the sugar, jelly and soy sauce and bring to the boil. Simmer for 5
minutes. Add the vinegar. Serve the pork on a bed of cooked
noodles, topped with the sauce.

Orange Chop

1 pork loin chop
½ oz. (2 T) flour
½ oz. (1 T) butter
½ small onion, sliced
¼ green pepper, cored, seeded and
  chopped

2 teaspoons brown sugar
¾ teaspoon made mustard
¼ pint (⅔ cup) unsweetened
  orange juice
½ orange, peeled and sliced

Coat the chop in the flour, then fry in the butter in a frying pan
(skillet) until browned on both sides. Remove the chop, then fry the
onion until tender. Add the green pepper, sugar and mustard, then
stir in the orange juice. Return the chop to the pan, cover and
simmer for 30 minutes. Add the orange slices halfway through the
cooking. Serve hot, with fresh vegetables in season.

SWEET AND SOUR PORK SLICES
(Photograph: Meat Promotion Executive)

Gammon (Ham) with Sweet and Sour Topping

1 small onion, chopped
1 small eating apple, peeled, cored and chopped
½ oz. (1 T) butter

1 teaspoon honey
1 tablespoon bottled brown sauce
1 gammon steak (ham slice)

Cook the onion and apple in the butter in a small saucepan for 5 minutes or until the onion is tender. Stir in the honey and sauce. Remove the rind from the gammon (ham) and make small cuts around the edge to prevent it curling. Place the gammon (ham) on a piece of foil and pile the apple mixture on top. Wrap loosely, sealing the edges well. Place on a baking sheet. Bake in a moderate oven, 350°F, Gas Mark 4 for 20 minutes. Remove from the foil and serve hot with vegetables in season.

Gammon (Ham) and Apricot Parcel

4 canned apricot halves, chopped
2 slices of brown bread, made into breadcrumbs
1 tablespoon chopped parsley

salt and pepper
1 gammon steak (ham slice), rind removed
2 tablespoons apricot can syrup

Mix together the apricots, breadcrumbs, parsley, salt and pepper. Put the apricot stuffing mixture on half of the gammon steak (ham slice) and fold the other half over the stuffing. Secure with a wooden cocktail stick if necessary.

Place the gammon (ham) parcel in a shallow ovenproof dish and pour over the apricot syrup. Cover the dish. Bake in a moderate oven, 350°F, Gas Mark 4 for 20 minutes or until the gammon (ham) is cooked and golden.

Note: The leftover apricots may be used in another dish or served with cream for dessert.

Scrambled Quickie

11 oz. (1 1/2 cups) frozen spinach
1/2 small onion, chopped
3 streaky bacon rashers (slices),
  chopped

2 oz. (1/4 cup) butter
2 eggs
1 tablespoon milk
salt and pepper

Cook the spinach according to directions on the pack. Fry the onion and bacon in half the butter in a small frying pan (skillet) until tender. Beat together the eggs, milk, salt and pepper. Melt 1/2 oz. (1T) of the remaining butter in a saucepan and stir in the egg mixture. Cook until light and creamy.

Heat the spinach in the remaining butter. Season to taste and arrange in a circle on a warmed serving plate. Turn the scrambled egg mixture into the centre of the spinach, sprinkle over the onion and bacon and serve immediately.

Sweet and Sour Chicken

2 oz. (1/4 cup) butter
salt and pepper
1 chicken joint (piece)
1 tablespoon cornflour (cornstarch)
1 tablespoon brown sugar
2 1/2 tablespoons malt vinegar

1/4 pint (2/3 cup) chicken stock
1 teaspoon soy sauce
1 tablespoon tomato ketchup
3 small slices of canned pineapple,
  chopped
freshly cooked rice

Melt the butter in a small frying pan (skillet). Season the chicken and fry gently in the butter for about 12 minutes on each side. Meanwhile, mix together the cornflour (cornstarch), sugar, salt, pepper, vinegar, stock and soy sauce in a saucepan. Stir over gentle heat until boiling. Add the ketchup and pineapple and simmer for about 3 minutes. Put the chicken on a warm plate, pour the sauce over and surround with cooked rice. Serve hot.

Chicken in a Foil Parcel

1 small onion, sliced into rings　　*salt and pepper*
1 celery stalk, chopped　　*pinch of dried tarragon*
1 small carrot, parboiled and sliced　　*2 tablespoons red wine*
1 chicken quarter

Put the onion, celery and carrot on a large piece of aluminium foil. Place the chicken on top. Season with salt and pepper, sprinkle with tarragon and pour the wine over. Secure the foil loosely around the chicken and place the parcel on a baking sheet. Bake in a moderately hot oven, 375°F, Gas Mark 5 for 45 minutes, opening the parcel about 10 minutes before the end of the cooking time so that the chicken can brown. Serve the chicken and vegetables on a warm serving plate, with vegetables in season.

Chicken with Barbecue Topping

1 chicken joint (piece)　　*1 teaspoon brown sugar*
1 oz. (2 T) butter　　*1 tablespoon bottled brown sauce*
1 tomato, skinned　　*salt and pepper*
1 small onion, chopped

Put the chicken in a small roasting tin, dot with half of the butter and bake in a moderately hot oven, 400°F, Gas Mark 6 for 20 minutes. Meanwhile, melt the remaining butter in a small saucepan. Add the tomato, onion, sugar, sauce, salt and pepper. Cover the pan and cook gently for 5 minutes.

Spoon this mixture over the chicken and return it to the oven. Bake for a further 20–30 minutes, basting frequently with the tomato mixture. Serve hot, with vegetables of your choice.

Turkey Chow Mein

4 oz. (½ cup) cooked turkey, cut
  into pieces
¼ pint (⅔ cup) thick chicken soup
2 teaspoons soy sauce
pinch of ground ginger
pinch of pepper
½ small onion, sliced
pinch of garlic salt
oil for frying

1 celery stalk, sliced
¼ green pepper, cored, seeded and
  thinly sliced
2 teaspoons cornflour (cornstarch)
4 oz. (½ cup) fresh bean sprouts or
  ½ small can
3 mushrooms, sliced
freshly cooked rice

Mix together the turkey meat, chicken soup, soy sauce, ground
ginger and pepper, then set aside. Gently fry the onion with the
garlic salt in the oil for 3 minutes or until tender. Add the celery,
green pepper and some of the soup from the turkey mixture. Heat to
almost boiling, then cover and simmer for 2-3 minutes.

Drain the turkey from the remaining soup, reserving the soup, and
add the turkey to the vegetables. Dissolve the cornflour (cornstarch)
in the reserved soup and add to the turkey mixture. Stir in the bean
sprouts and mushrooms. Cover and cook for a further 5-10 minutes
or until all the ingredients are heated through. Served hot with
freshly cooked rice.

Mixed Grill

oil
salt and pepper
4 oz. rump (boneless sirloin) steak
1 lamb's kidney, skinned, cored and
  halved

1 small tomato, halved
1 streaky bacon rasher (slice)
2 mushrooms
watercress to garnish

Heat the grill (broiler) and brush the rack and all ingredients with a little oil. Season all ingredients with salt and pepper. Grill (broil) the steak for 2 minutes on one side, then turn and add the kidney, tomato and bacon. Grill (broil) for 4 minutes, turning once. Add the mushrooms and grill (broil) for a further 5 minutes, turning the other ingredients as necessary. Serve on a heated plate, garnished with watercress.

Liver with Orange

1 small onion, chopped
oil for frying
1/4 pint (2/3 cup) stock, made from
  yeast (meat) extract
grated rind and juice of 1 small
  orange

salt and pepper
4 oz. ox (beef) liver, thinly sliced
chopped parsley to garnish

Fry the onion in the oil until tender. Stir in the stock, orange rind and juice, salt and pepper and bring to the boil. Add the liver. Simmer gently for 8-10 minutes or until the liver is cooked. Spoon onto a warm plate, garnish with parsley and serve hot with mashed potatoes and vegetables in season.

Liver and Bacon Casserole

6 oz. ox (beef) liver, sliced, soaked
  in milk for 1 hour and drained
flour
salt and pepper
½ small onion, chopped
½ oz. (1 T) butter

2 canned tomatoes plus 2
  tablespoons can juice
2 teaspoons tomato purée (paste)
1 streaky bacon rasher (slice),
  halved and rolled

Coat the liver in a little flour seasoned with salt and pepper. Fry the
onion in the butter until soft. Add the liver and fry on both sides
until browned. Put the liver and onions in a small ovenproof
casserole and season with salt and pepper. Chop the tomatoes
roughly and add to the casserole together with the juice and tomato
purée (paste). Top with the bacon rolls and bake in a moderately hot
oven, 375°F, Gas Mark 5 for 30 minutes. Serve hot with boiled
potatoes and a green vegetable.

Liver Stroganoff

4 oz. pig's (pork) liver
½ oz. (1 T) butter
½ small onion, sliced
¼ green pepper, cored, seeded and
  sliced
2 mushrooms, sliced

1 teaspoon flour
¼ pint (⅔ cup) stock
1 teaspoon tomato purée (paste)
pinch of sugar
1 tablespoon single (light) cream
freshly boiled rice

Cut the liver into short narrow strips, then fry in the butter for 1-2
minutes. Drain and keep warm. Add the vegetables to the butter in
the pan and fry for about 2 minutes. Stir in the flour. Mix together
the stock, tomato purée (paste) and sugar and gradually add to the
pan. Stir well and add the liver. Bring to the boil and simmer for 15
minutes. Stir in the cream and reheat carefully. Pour into a serving
dish and surround with freshly boiled rice. Serve hot.

Liver Paupiettes

2 lean bacon rashers (slices)
2 thin slices calf's liver
salt and pepper
1 1/2 teaspoons lemon juice
2 sprigs of thyme
1 oz. (2 T) butter

1 teaspoon flour
2 tablespoons Marsala
1 tomato, skinned and chopped
1 1/2 tablespoons beef stock
lemon slices to garnish

Place the bacon slices on the liver and season with salt and pepper. Sprinkle over the lemon juice and put a thyme sprig in the centre of each slice. Roll up the slices and secure them with wooden cocktail sticks.

Melt the butter in a frying pan (skillet). Add the liver rolls and fry for 4 minutes. Stir in the flour to form a smooth paste with the butter. Gradually stir in the Marsala and bring to the boil. Add the tomato and stock and stir to mix. Cover and simmer for 8 minutes, or until the liver rolls are cooked through. Garnish with lemon slices.

Kidneys with Mustard Sauce

1/2 oz. (1 T) butter
2 lamb's kidneys, skinned, halved
  and cored
1/2 small onion, sliced
2 oz. (1/2 cup) mushrooms, sliced
1 teaspoon French mustard

1 tablespoon milk
1 tablespoon single (light) cream
pinch of grated nutmeg
salt and pepper
chopped parsley to garnish

Melt the butter in a saucepan, add the kidneys and cook until tender. Remove from the pan and keep warm.

Add the onion and mushrooms to the pan, cook for 5 minutes, then stir in the mustard, milk and cream. Return the kidneys to the pan, add nutmeg and seasoning to taste, then reheat to just below boiling point.

Serve sprinkled with chopped parsley.

Devilled Kidneys

1 small onion, chopped
1 small carrot, diced
1 streaky bacon rasher (slice),
  chopped
½ oz. (1 T) butter
2-3 lambs' kidneys, skinned,
  halved and cored

1 tablespoon flour
¼ pint (⅔ cup) stock
1 teaspoon French mustard
2 tablespoons tomato ketchup
1 teaspoon bottled brown sauce
2 mushrooms, quartered
salt and pepper

Cook the onion, carrot and bacon in the butter in a saucepan until tender. Add the kidneys and brown on all sides. Stir in the flour and cook for 1 minute. Remove from the heat and carefully stir in the stock, mustard, ketchup, brown sauce, mushrooms, salt and pepper. Return to the heat and bring to the boil, stirring all the time. Cover and simmer for about 15 minutes until the kidneys are tender. Serve hot with boiled rice or noodles.

Casseroled Heart

2 tablespoons oil
1 small onion, chopped
1 streaky bacon rasher (slice),
  chopped
2 mushrooms, sliced
1 lamb's heart, cleaned

½ oz. (2 T) flour
½ packet dry spring vegetable soup
  mix
¾ pint (2 cups) water
½ beef stock (1 bouillon) cube

Heat the oil in a saucepan and fry the onion until tender. Mix together the bacon and mushrooms and use to stuff the heart. Fry the heart on all sides until brown, then drain. Add the flour to the juices in the pan and cook for 1 minute. Gradually stir in the soup mix and water. Crumble in the stock (bouillon) cube, then return the heart to the pan. Bring to the boil, cover and simmer for 1¼ hours or until the heart is tender. Serve hot with cooked rice or pasta.

INTERESTING WAYS WITH VEGETABLES AND SALADS

Breda Stuffed Cabbage

4 oz. (½ cup) chicken livers,
  chopped
½ onion, finely chopped
1 streaky bacon rasher (slice),
  chopped
½ oz. (1 T) unsalted butter
1 tablespoon tomato purée (paste)
½ teaspoon dried oregano
½ teaspoon dried mixed herbs

salt and pepper
3 oz. Edam cheese, cut into 2 slices
2 large cabbage leaves, blanched
  and drained, or 4 canned vine
  leaves
4 oz. (½ cup) canned tomatoes,
  pressed through a sieve (strainer)
1 teaspoon cornflour (cornstarch)
plain yogurt

Fry the chicken livers, onion and bacon in the butter in a frying pan
(skillet) for 10 minutes. Stir in the tomato purée (paste), herbs, salt
and pepper and simmer gently for 5 minutes.

Place a slice of cheese on each cabbage leaf and put half of the
filling on top of each. Fold up the leaves to enclose the filling and
place the parcels in an ovenproof dish. Mix together the canned
tomatoes and cornflour (cornstarch) and bring to the boil, stirring all
the time. Pour over the cabbage parcels. Bake in a moderately hot
oven, 375°F, Gas Mark 5 for 25 minutes. Serve hot with yogurt.

Alternatively, divide the filling between 4 vine leaves and cook in
the same way.

BREDA STUFFED CABBAGE

Cottage Pepper Slices

4 oz. (½ cup) cottage cheese
2 oz. (¼ cup) cream cheese
chopped parsley or chives

1 green or red pepper
paprika

Mix together the cottage cheese, cream cheese and chopped parsley or chives. Remove the stalk end from the pepper, then remove the seeds. Fill the pepper with the cheese mixture. Put it in a covered dish in the refrigerator and leave overnight, or for at least 3 hours. Cut into thick slices and sprinkle each with paprika. Serve with a selection of cold meats.

Spiced Carrots

4 oz. (¾ cup) carrots, sliced
½ oz. (1 T) butter, melted
1 tablespoon orange juice
¼ teaspoon grated orange rind

pinch of ground ginger
pinch of grated nutmeg
salt and pepper
chopped parsley to garnish

Put the carrots in a small ovenproof dish. Mix together the remaining ingredients, except the parsley, and spoon over the carrots.

Cover and cook in a moderately hot oven, 375°F, Gas Mark 5 for 25 minutes. Sprinkle with parsley just before serving.

Beef-stuffed Onion

3 oz. (⅓ cup) cooked minced
  (ground) beef
1 oz. (2 T) butter, melted
1 oz. (½ cup) breadcrumbs

pinch of dried sage
1 teaspoon chopped parsley
salt and pepper
1 very large onion

Place the minced (ground) beef in a bowl and add half the butter, the breadcrumbs and herbs. Mix well and season with salt and pepper to taste.

Boil the onion in salted water for 30 minutes, or until the outside is tender. Drain and cool. Carefully scoop out the centre of the onion. Chop the flesh coarsely and add to the meat mixture.

Brush the bottom of a small ovenproof dish with some of the remaining melted butter and put the onion shell in the dish. Spoon the meat mixture into the onion, piling it quite high. Pour the remaining butter over the top. Put the dish into a moderate oven, 350°F, Gas Mark 4 and bake for 1 hour.

If the stuffing becomes too brown, cover the dish with foil.

Glazed Onions

4 oz. (1 cup) small pickling (pearl)
  onions
1 oz. (2 T) butter

1 oz. (2 T) caster sugar
salt and pepper

Put the onions in a saucepan with the butter, sugar, salt and pepper.
Cover the pan and cook very gently, shaking the pan from time to
time, until the onions are tender and glazed. Serve hot with cooked
meat dishes, such as fried or grilled (broiled) liver or a lamb chop.

Sweet Buttered Parsnips

4 oz. parsnips, roughly chopped
1 oz. (2 T) butter

brown sugar

Cook the parsnips by steaming or boiling. Drain. Melt the butter in a
saucepan, add the parsnips and toss very carefully together. Sprinkle
with sugar to taste and serve hot, with meat dishes.

Zildijk Casserole

1 small carrot, sliced
1 small courgette (zucchini), sliced
½ medium onion, sliced
few florets of cauliflower
2 small leaves of white cabbage,
  shredded
2 oz. (¼ cup) cooked spinach
½ oz. (1 T) butter

½ oz. (2 T) flour
3 tablespoons low-fat reconstituted
  milk
2 oz. (½ cup) Edam cheese, finely
  grated
salt and pepper
1 tablespoon fresh breadcrumbs

Blanch the carrot, courgette (zucchini), onion, cauliflower and cabbage in boiling water for 3 minutes. Drain, reserving 3 tablespoons of the liquid, and place the vegetables in an ovenproof dish. Cover with the cooked spinach.

Melt the butter in a saucepan. Stir in the flour and cook for 1 minute. Gradually stir in the milk and reserved liquid and cook, stirring, until the sauce becomes thick. Stir in half the cheese and salt and pepper to taste. Pour the sauce over the vegetables.

Sprinkle the remaining cheese and the breadcrumbs over the surface. Bake in a moderately hot oven, 375°F, Gas Mark 5 for 30 minutes. Serve hot.

Crunchy Leek Bake

2 medium-sized leeks
salt and pepper
2 streaky bacon rashers (slices)
1 oz. (2 T) butter

1 oz. (½ cup) fresh breadcrumbs
1 oz. (¼ cup) Cheddar cheese,
  grated

Cut the leeks into pieces about 6 inches long and wash them thoroughly. Blanch in boiling, salted water for about 5 minutes. Drain well. Wrap a rasher (slice) of bacon around each leek and place in a well-greased ovenproof dish. Season with salt and pepper. Melt the butter, add to the breadcrumbs and grated cheese and sprinkle over the leeks in the dish. Bake in a moderately hot oven, 375°F, Gas Mark 5 for 40–50 minutes or until the leeks are tender and the topping is golden brown. Serve hot. This is not only a very tasty vegetable, but may also be served as a snack in itself.

ZILDIJK CASSEROLE
(Photograph: Dutch Dairy Bureau)

Mushrooms with Parsley Butter

1 oz. (2 T) butter
4 oz. (1 cup) button mushrooms,
  halved
salt and pepper

pinch of grated nutmeg
1 teaspoon chopped parsley
pinch of cayenne pepper
1 teaspoon lemon juice

Melt half of the butter in a saucepan. Add the mushrooms, salt,
pepper and nutmeg and cook gently for 5 minutes. Work the
remaining butter to soften it, then add the remaining ingredients.
Add this parsley butter to the mushrooms in the pan and serve hot.
This is ideal with fish dishes and sausages.

Prune-stuffed Tomatoes

2 large firm tomatoes
1 oz. (2 T) butter
1 oz. (2 T) cream cheese

4 canned prunes, chopped
2 walnut halves
few lettuce leaves

Cut a circle, about 1¼ inches across, from the top of each tomato.
Scoop out the inside using a teaspoon and turn the shells upside
down to drain. Cream together the butter and cream cheese, then
add the chopped prunes. Mix thoroughly and fill the shells with the
prune mixture. Top each with a walnut half and the tomato top, then
sit them on a bed of lettuce. This is a nice change from a green salad
to serve with cold cooked meats, or with cooked fish dishes.

Cauliflower Cheese

3 florets of cauliflower
¼ oz. (2 T) butter
¼ oz. (1 T) flour
¼ pint (⅔ cup) milk
paprika

½ teaspoon French mustard
2 oz. (½ cup) Cheddar cheese,
  finely grated
2 digestive biscuits (graham
  crackers), finely crushed

Cook the cauliflower in boiling salted water until tender. Drain. Melt the butter in a saucepan, add the flour and cook for 1 minute. Gradually stir in the milk and bring to the boil. Add paprika and the French mustard and simmer for 1 minute, stirring all the time.

Put the cooked cauliflower in a warmed heatproof serving dish and cover with the sauce. Sprinkle the grated cheese and crushed biscuits (crackers) over the surface. Brown under a hot grill (broiler). Serve hot with a grilled (broiled) chop or sausages, or with a fish dish.

Crunchy Potato Bakes

2-3 potatoes, cooked and mashed
salt and pepper
1 ½ tablespoons thick mayonnaise

beaten egg
2 oz. (½ cup) blanched almonds,
  roughly chopped

Place the mashed potatoes in a bowl, add salt, pepper and mayonnaise and mix well. Roll the mixture into 2 or 3 croquette shapes. Brush with a little beaten egg and dip in the almonds to coat each croquette thoroughly. Bake in a moderate oven, 350°F, Gas Mark 4 for 30 minutes. Serve hot as an accompaniment to chicken and fish dishes.

Rice Ratatouille

1 courgette (zucchini), cut into
  ¼ inch slices
1 small aubergine (eggplant), cut
  into ¼ inch slices
salt and pepper
2 tablespoons oil
¼ green pepper, cored, seeded and
  sliced

½ small onion, chopped
½ garlic clove, crushed
1 tomato, chopped
2 oz. (¼ cup) long-grain rice
¼ pint (⅔ cup) stock, made by
  dissolving ¼ stock (½ bouillon)
  cube in boiling water

Put the courgette (zucchini) and aubergine (eggplant) slices in a colander. Sprinkle with salt and leave for 30 minutes to drain. Rinse.

   Heat the oil in a large saucepan. Add the green pepper, onion, garlic, tomato, courgette (zucchini) and aubergine (eggplant). Fry gently together for about 10 minutes. Add the rice, stock, salt and pepper. Cover the pan and simmer for 25 minutes or until the rice has absorbed the liquid and the vegetables are tender. Serve hot, with a grilled (broiled) chop or baked fish.

Prawn (Shrimp), Rice and Tomato Salad

1 oz. (2 T) long-grain rice
2 tablespoons salad cream
  (mayonnaise)
1 tablespoon tomato ketchup
1 tablespoon canned sweetcorn
  kernels, drained

2 oz. (⅓ cup) shelled prawns
  (shrimp)
½ inch piece of cucumber, chopped
1 tablespoon sultanas (seedless
  white raisins)
paprika

Cook the rice in boiling salted water until just tender. Rinse in cold water, then leave until cold. Mix together the salad cream (mayonnaise) and tomato ketchup, then stir in the remaining ingredients, including the rice. Serve on a flat platter, with hard-boiled egg slices, or cold meat.

RICE RATATOUILLE
(Photograph: Knorr Stock Cubes)

Chicken, Avocado and Grapefruit Salad

4 oz. (½ cup) cooked chicken
  meat, diced
1 oz. (2 T) long-grain rice, cooked
½ grapefruit, peeled and segmented
onion salt
1 small carrot, cut into sticks
salt and pepper
½ avocado, peeled and diced

few drops of lemon juice
2 tablespoons French dressing
Chinese leaves (bok choy) or
  lettuce
watercress
2 tablespoons thick mayonnaise
½ teaspoon curry powder

Put the chicken in a bowl with the rice, grapefruit, onion salt, carrot
sticks, salt and pepper. Coat the avocado dice with the lemon juice to
prevent discoloration, then add to the bowl with the French dressing.
Toss well together.

Arrange a bed of Chinese leaves (bok choy) or lettuce and
watercress on a flat plate. Pile the salad on top. Mix together the
mayonnaise and curry powder and spoon on top. Serve chilled, with
brown bread and butter. This salad is a complete meal in itself.
Note: The remaining ½ avocado should be immediately brushed on
the cut surface with lemon juice and then tightly wrapped in cling
film (plastic wrap). Use the next day.

Ogen Chicken Salad

½ small Ogen (cantaloupe) melon
4 slices of cooked chicken breast
½ green pepper, cored, seeded and
  chopped

1 oz. (¼ cup) walnuts, roughly
  chopped
2 tablespoons thick mayonnaise
chopped parsley to garnish

Remove the seeds from the melon. Scoop out the flesh with a melon
baller or chop it and place in a bowl. Cut the chicken meat into
bite-sized pieces and add to the bowl, together with the green pepper
and walnuts. Stir in the mayonnaise and mix thoroughly. Scatter
chopped parsley over the surface, then serve. This is a refreshing
salad, which can be served on its own or with hard-boiled egg.

Jaffa Tomato

2 tomatoes, thinly sliced
1 tablespoon orange juice
1 teaspoon caster sugar

1 celery stalk, finely chopped
½ small onion, sliced into rings
parsley sprigs to garnish

Arrange the tomato slices on a plate. Pour over the orange juice and sprinkle with the sugar. Chill in the refrigerator for 1 hour. Scatter the celery and onion over the tomatoes and garnish with sprigs of parsley. This is ideal to serve with grilled (broiled) steak, chops or sausages.

Last Minute Salad

few lettuce leaves
1 orange, peeled and segmented
few slices of pickled beetroot (beet),
   chopped
2 tablespoons olive oil

2 teaspoons wine vinegar
1 teaspoon caster sugar
salt and pepper
few toasted split almonds

Arrange lettuce leaves in the bottom of a small salad bowl, then place the orange segments and chopped beetroot (beet) on top. Shake the oil, vinegar, sugar, salt and pepper in a screwtop jar until well mixed. Pour this dressing over the salad and scatter the almonds on top. Serve with cold cooked meats.

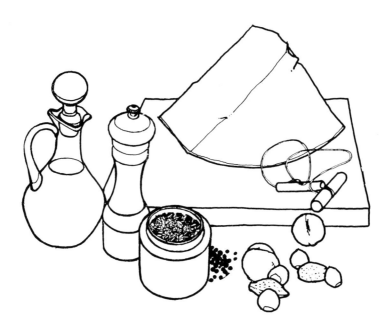

SNACKS AND SUPPER DISHES

Buck Rarebit

2 oz. (½ cup) Cheddar cheese,
  grated
1 oz. (2 T) butter
2 eggs

salt and pepper
1 tablespoon beer or milk
little made mustard
1 slice of bread

Mix together the cheese, half of the butter, 1 egg, beaten, salt and
pepper. Stir in the beer or milk and mustard. Toast the bread on one
side. Turn over and lightly toast the other side. Spread the remaining
butter on the toast and top with the cheese mixture. Grill (broil)
slowly until golden. Meanwhile, poach the remaining egg in gently
simmering water. Drain. Place the poached egg on top of the rarebit.
Serve hot.

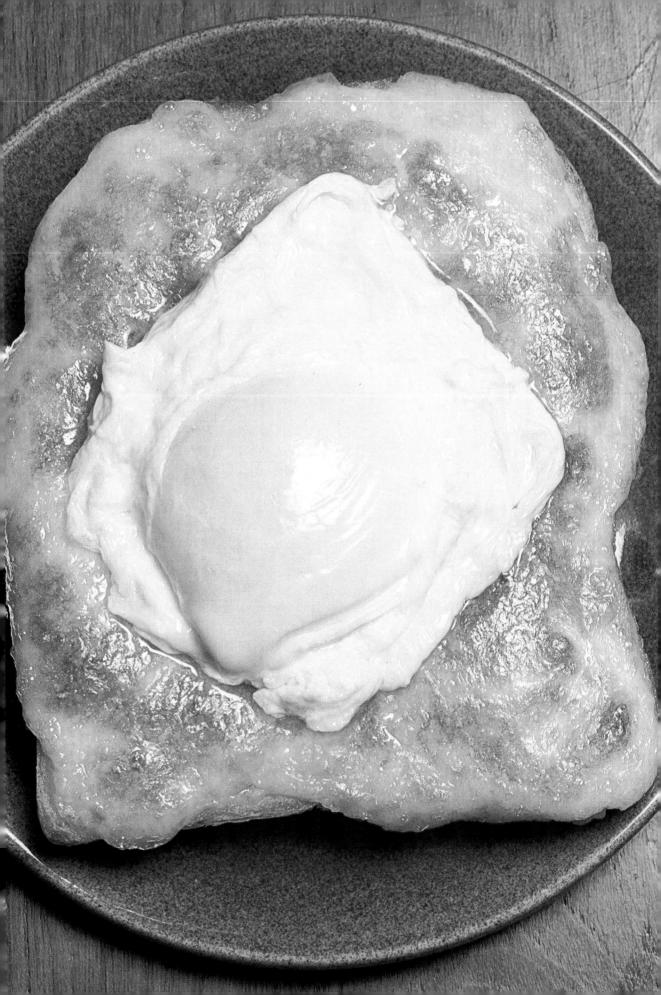

Bean Omelette

3 eggs, separated
salt and pepper
½ oz. (1 T) butter
7 oz. (1 cup) canned baked beans
 in tomato sauce

2 oz. (⅓ cup) shelled prawns
 (shrimp)

Beat the egg yolks with salt and pepper. Beat the egg whites until stiff and fold into the yolks. Melt the butter in an omelette pan. Pour in the egg mixture and cook until the bottom is set.

Meanwhile, heat together the baked beans and prawns (shrimp) in a saucepan. Place the omelette under a hot grill (broiler) to allow the top to set and puff up. Turn the omelette onto a warm plate and fill with the beans and prawns (shrimp). Fold the omelette over the filling and slit the top. Serve immediately.

Tuna Pâté Toasts

3½ oz. (½ cup) canned tuna fish,
 flaked
1 hard-boiled egg, finely chopped
4 oz. (½ cup) cream cheese
few snipped chives

salt and pepper
few sprigs of parsley, chopped
1 tablespoon brandy (optional)
hot buttered toast

Mash together the tuna fish and egg. Gradually work in the cream cheese, chives, salt, pepper, parsley and brandy, if used. Mix very thoroughly. (If a blender is available, place the mixture in this and blend together for a few seconds.) Spoon the mixture into a small ramekin dish and chill in the refrigerator. Serve with hot buttered toast, cut into fingers. This also makes a delightful appetizer to a main meal.

Beef and Rice Croquettes

4 oz. (½ cup) minced (ground)
  beef
1½ oz. (¼ cup) long-grain rice,
  cooked
1 small onion, finely chopped
½ small can condensed vegetable
  soup

salt and pepper
beaten egg
golden breadcrumbs
oil for deep frying

Mix together the beef, rice and onion and bind together with a little of the condensed soup. Add salt and pepper to taste. Divide into two and shape into croquettes on a floured board. Brush each with beaten egg, then coat in breadcrumbs.

Deep fry for about 10–15 minutes until golden brown. Drain well. Heat the remaining soup with a little water in a saucepan and serve as a rich sauce over the croquettes. These croquettes are delicious with a green salad.

Danish Open Sandwiches

Businessman's Bite Cover a slice of buttered bread with lettuce, lay a slice of liver pâté on top, then place a rasher (slice) of crisply fried bacon diagonally across the sandwich. Garnish the centre with a tomato twist and gherkin (dill pickle) fan.

Tivoli Special Cover a slice of buttered bread with lettuce. Arrange slices of hard-boiled egg in two rows on top. Spoon thick mayonnaise along the centre and sprinkle with Danish-style caviar. Garnish with a sprig of parsley.

Russian Roulette Roll up two slices of cooked ham and place diagonally across a slice of buttered bread. Place 1 tablespoon of Russian salad on one corner and a twist of cucumber at the other. Garnish the ham with radish roses and watercress.

Beefeater's Lunch Cover a slice of buttered bread with lettuce. Fold two thin slices of roast beef in half and place on top. Place a prune and a tomato slice at one corner, with a sprig of parsley in between. Spoon a few slices of cooked mushroom over part of the tomato and place 2 spring onions (scallions) over the beef.

Lover's Lament Cover a slice of buttered bread with lettuce. Twist three slices of salami into cornets and position, pointing outwards, in the corner. Place 1 tablespoon of thick mayonnaise in the corner. Top the salami with onion rings and garnish with stuffed olives and watercress.

Simple Simon Overlap three slices of Esrom cheese on a slice of buttered bread. Place two thin slices of eating apple between the cheese slices in one corner and garnish the opposite corner with a twist of orange and watercress.

DANISH OPEN SANDWICHES
(Photograph: Carlsberg)

Cheese and Bacon Macaroni

2 oz. (½ cup) macaroni
3 streaky bacon rashers (slices)
1 teaspoon cornflour (cornstarch)
¼ pint (⅔ cup) milk
1 oz. (¼ cup) Cheddar cheese,
  grated

salt and pepper
pinch of dry mustard
1 teaspoon yeast (meat) extract

Cook the macaroni in boiling salted water for 15 minutes or until tender. Meanwhile, grill (broil) the bacon until crisp. Drain the bacon and macaroni. Mix together the cornflour (cornstarch) and milk in a small saucepan and bring to the boil, stirring constantly. Stir in the macaroni, cheese, salt, pepper, mustard and yeast (meat) extract. Crumble in the bacon. Place in a serving dish and serve immediately.

Cheesy Rice

3 oz. (½ cup) long-grain rice
1 celery stalk, finely chopped
leftover cooked vegetables
½ tablespoon corn oil

3 oz. (¾ cup) Cheddar cheese,
  grated
salt and pepper

Cook the rice in boiling salted water until tender. Meanwhile, heat the vegetables, including the celery, in a little boiling water. Drain. Mix the vegetables and rice together and stir in the oil, grated cheese, salt and pepper. Serve immediately on a warm plate.

Crispy Pork and Ham Fingers

½ small can chopped pork and ham
beaten egg
4 tablespoons (¼ cup) oatmeal

oil for frying
cranberry sauce

Cut the ham and pork into two fingers and dip these in the beaten egg. Roll each in oatmeal. Fry in hot shallow oil until golden and crisp. Drain thoroughly and serve hot, with cranberry sauce.

Ham and Banana Savoury

1 oz. (2 T) butter
2 small bananas, sliced
2 slices of cooked ham
½ oz. (2 T) flour

¼ pint (⅔ cup) milk
salt and pepper
2 oz. (½ cup) Cheddar cheese,
 grated

Melt half of the butter in a saucepan. Brush the bananas with the
melted butter and grill (broil) gently until hot. Place one slice of ham
on the bottom of a flameproof dish. Add the banana slices and top
with the second slice of ham.

Melt the remaining butter in the saucepan. Add the flour and cook
for 1 minute. Gradually stir in the milk and bring to the boil, stirring
constantly. Stir in salt, pepper and the cheese. Pour this sauce over
the ham and place the dish under a hot grill (broiler) to heat through.
Serve immediately, with a roll and butter if liked.

Fish Soufflé

6 oz. packet frozen cod in shrimp
  sauce

1 egg, separated
salt and pepper

Cook the fish according to the instructions on the packet. While still hot, turn into a bowl and mix in the egg yolk. Beat the egg white until stiff and fold carefully into the mixture. Season with salt and pepper, and spoon into a small soufflé dish. Bake in a moderately hot oven, 375°F, Gas Mark 5 for 15-20 minutes or until golden brown. Serve immediately.

Seafood Scallop

shortcrust (pie) pastry, made with
  3 oz. (¾ cup) flour, etc.
½ oz. (1 T) butter
½ oz. (2 T) flour
4 fl. oz. (½ cup) milk
onion salt
pinch of dried mixed herbs
salt and pepper
1 tablespoon double (heavy) cream
1 egg yolk

1 bacon rasher (slice), chopped
3-4 button mushrooms, sliced
4 oz. (½ cup) cooked white fish,
  e.g. cod, haddock or coley,
  skinned and boned (if necessary)
  and flaked
2 teaspoons sherry
1 oz. (2½ T) fresh shelled prawns
  (shrimp)
parsley sprigs to garnish

Roll out the dough and use to line a large scallop shell or individual ovenproof dish. Trim the edges and bake blind in a moderately hot oven, 400°F, Gas Mark 6 for 15 minutes or until crisp and brown.

    Put the butter, flour, milk, onion salt, mixed herbs, salt and pepper in a saucepan. Heat, whisking constantly, until the sauce comes to the boil. Stir in the cream and egg yolk and keep warm. Meanwhile, fry together the bacon and mushrooms until lightly cooked. Add the fish to the sauce together with the sherry and pour into the prepared pie case. Scatter the bacon, mushrooms and prawns (shrimp) on top. Garnish with parsley and serve hot.

Chickenburger

1 chicken leg
1 tomato, sliced
1 small onion, sliced
½ oz. (1 T) butter

freshly ground black pepper
1 hamburger bun, split
lettuce leaves to garnish

Remove the meat from the chicken leg. Discard the skin and mince (grind) the flesh finely. Shape the minced (ground) chicken into a patty and place in the refrigerator to become firm. Meanwhile, heat the tomato and onion slices in the butter in a saucepan. Sprinkle pepper over the chickenburger and grill (broil) for 5-7 minutes on each side, until cooked and golden. Place in the bun and top with the tomato and onion mixture. Garnish with lettuce leaves and serve hot.

Beefburger Bake

2 frozen beefburgers (hamburgers)
1 small onion, sliced
1 tomato, sliced

3 mushrooms, sliced
½ oz. (1 T) butter
salt and pepper

Place the burgers in an ovenproof dish. Scatter the onion rings, tomato slices and sliced mushrooms on top. Top with the butter. Season with salt and pepper, cover the dish and bake in a moderately hot oven, 375°F, Gas Mark 5 for 30 minutes. Serve hot.

Sausage and Bacon Burger

½ small onion, finely chopped
½ oz. (1 T) butter
4 oz. (½ cup) pork sausagemeat
1 streaky bacon rasher (slice),
  chopped

½ teaspoon gravy powder
pinch of dried mixed herbs
flour
oil for frying

Lightly fry the onion in the butter for 2-3 minutes until soft. Put the onion into a bowl and add the sausagemeat, bacon, gravy powder and mixed herbs. Mix well, then shape the mixture into a burger. Chill in the refrigerator until firm. Coat the burger in flour, then fry in shallow oil for 4 minutes on each side, until crisp and golden brown. Serve either in a toasted bun or with a salad.

Bacon and Cheese Rösti

8 oz. medium-sized old potatoes,
  peeled and halved
4 streaky bacon rashers (slices),
  chopped

1 small onion, thinly sliced
2 oz. (½ cup) Cheddar cheese, cut
  into small cubes
salt and pepper

Cook the potatoes in boiling salted water for 5 minutes. Drain. Fry the bacon and onion in a frying pan (skillet) until golden. Grate the potatoes coarsely into the pan. Add the cubed cheese, salt and pepper. Smooth the surface and cook until the bottom is crisp and brown—about 5 minutes. Place under a hot grill (broiler) to cook the top. Serve immediately, with a sauce of your choice.

Pizza Bonanza

1 small onion, sliced
1 oz. (2 T) butter
2 oz. (½ cup) mushrooms, sliced
5 oz. white bread mix
2 tablespoons tomato purée (paste)
4 oz. frozen spinach, thawed and
  drained

2 oz. (¼ cup) garlic sausage,
  thinly sliced
salt and pepper
2 oz. (½ cup) cheese, grated

Sauté the onions in half of the butter, until golden, then remove from the pan. Sauté the mushrooms in the remaining butter until softened.

Make up the bread mix with hot water, according to the packet instructions. Knead for 5 minutes, then roll out to a rectangle, about 10 × 6 inches. Transfer to a lightly greased baking sheet and lightly mark into four sections, using the point of a knife. Spread the tomato purée (paste) over the dough. Place the mushrooms on one quarter, the onions on another, the spinach on the third quarter and the garlic sausage on the remaining section. Season with salt and pepper, then sprinkle cheese over the top.

Bake in a moderately hot oven, 400°F, Gas Mark 6 for 15 minutes. Serve hot or cold.

Quick Portuguese Pizza

1 English muffin, split
tomato ketchup
2 canned sardines in oil
garlic salt

2 slices of processed cheese
pinch of dried oregano
2 black olives

Spread each muffin half with tomato ketchup. Top each with a sardine. Sprinkle with garlic salt, top with a slice of processed cheese, brush with some of the oil from the sardines, then sprinkle oregano over the surface. Garnish with the black olives. Place the pizzas under a hot grill (broiler) and grill (broil) until golden—about 15 minutes. Serve hot.

PIZZA BONANZA
(Photograph: Home Baking Bureau)

French Omelette

3 eggs
1 tablespoon cold water

salt and pepper
½ oz. (1 T) butter

Place a 7 inch omelette pan over the heat to get thoroughly hot. Beat the eggs in a bowl, add the water and seasoning and beat again. Put the butter in the pan to melt. When sizzling, pour in the beaten eggs. With a palette knife, draw the mixture from the sides of the pan into the middle, repeating this until all the egg has been cooked. Fold over one-half of the omelette, remove from the heat and tilt the pan to slide it out onto a warmed plate.

Vegetable Cannelloni

2 cannelloni tubes
salt
2 tomatoes, skinned and chopped
1 oz. (¼ cup) Cheddar cheese,
 grated
1 oz. (½ cup) fresh breadcrumbs

1 teaspoon chopped parsley
pepper
beaten egg
1 small can tomatoes
pinch of dried oregano

Plunge the cannelloni tubes in boiling salted water for 5 minutes or until just soft. Drain, rinse under cold running water, then drain again on paper towels.

Put the fresh tomatoes, cheese, breadcrumbs, parsley and seasoning in a bowl and stir well to mix. Bind the mixture with a little beaten egg. Fill the cannelloni tubes with this mixture and place in a small ovenproof dish.

Chop the canned tomatoes in their juice and pour over the cannelloni. Sprinkle with a little oregano and place in a moderate oven, 350°F, Gas Mark 4 for 30 minutes or until heated through.

Pork-stuffed Pepper

1 slice of cooked pork, finely
  chopped
1 oz. (2 T) pork sausagemeat
1 oz. (2 T) long-grain rice, cooked
1 tomato, chopped

1 large mushroom, chopped
salt and pepper
pinch of dried basil
1 large green pepper
oil

Mix together the meats, rice, tomato, mushroom, salt, pepper and
basil. Remove the top of the pepper and discard the seeds. Fill with
the meat mixture, replace the top and brush with oil. Place on a
baking sheet. Bake in a moderately hot oven, 375°F, Gas Mark 5 for
30-40 minutes. Serve hot or cold.

Ham and Pork Toppers

2 thick slices of canned chopped
  ham and pork, cubed
½ small can tomatoes
pinch of dried thyme

1 crusty bread roll, halved
1 oz. (¼ cup) Cheddar cheese,
  grated

Mix together the meat, tomatoes and thyme and pile on top of the
rolls. Sprinkle with the grated cheese. Cook under a hot grill
(broiler) for about 10 minutes or until bubbly. Serve hot.

DESSERTS

Cinnamon Pear Delight

1 pear, peeled, halved and cored
¼ pint (⅔ cup) dry (hard) cider
large pinch of ground cinnamon
1 tablespoon demerara (raw) sugar

little grated lemon rind
1-2 tablespoons double (heavy)
  cream, whipped
2 teaspoons chopped nuts

Place the pear, cider, cinnamon and sugar in a pan. Cover and simmer over a low heat for 10–15 minutes, until the pear is tender. Leave to cool. Fold the lemon rind into the whipped cream. Arrange the pear on a serving dish, decorate with whipped cream and sprinkle with chopped nuts.

Fruit Nut Sundae

2 individual tubs frozen chocolate
  mousse, thawed
2 tablespoons raisins

2 tablespoons flaked almonds
little grated plain (semisweet)
  chocolate

Mix together the mousse, raisins and flaked almonds. Spoon the mixture into a glass sundae dish, then decorate with grated chocolate. Chill in the refrigerator before serving.

CINNAMON PEAR DELIGHT
(Photograph: Taunton Cider)

Melon Sherry Cup

½ medium-sized Ogen
 (cantaloupe) melon
1 teaspoon finely grated orange rind

2 teaspoons medium sherry
2 maraschino cherries

Remove the seeds from the melon. Scoop out the flesh using a melon baller and place in a bowl. Add the orange rind and sherry and mix well. Return to the melon shell. Decorate with the cherries and chill before serving.

Strawberries Romanoff

4 oz. (¾ cup) strawberries, hulled
1 tablespoon brandy or orange
 liqueur
2½ tablespoons double (heavy)
 cream

few drops of vanilla essence
 (extract)

Put the strawberries in a glass dish and pour over the brandy or liqueur. Chill in the refrigerator for 1 hour.

Beat the cream and vanilla together until thick. Spoon over the strawberries and serve.

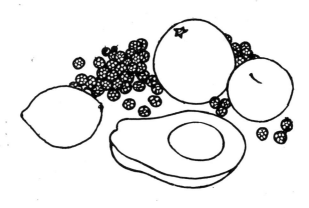

Chocolate Mousse

*1 oz. (1 square) plain (semisweet)
  chocolate*

*1 teaspoon cold water
1 egg, separated*

Melt the chocolate with the water in a heatproof bowl over a pan of hot water. Beat the egg yolk into the chocolate, then leave to cool. Beat the egg white until stiff and carefully fold into the chocolate mixture. Spoon into a stemmed glass and chill in the refrigerator before serving.

Semolina Soufflé

*1 tablespoon semolina (cream of
  wheat)
1 tablespoon cocoa powder
1 tablespoon caster sugar*

*⅓ pint (⅞ cup) milk
1 egg, separated
2 teaspoons chopped mixed nuts*

Place the semolina (cream of wheat), cocoa and sugar in a bowl and add enough milk to mix to a thin paste. Bring the remaining milk to the boil and stir into the mixture. Return to the pan and bring to the boil, stirring constantly. Simmer for 5 minutes. Cool. Add the egg yolk to the chocolate mixture. Beat the egg white until stiff. Carefully fold the egg white into the chocolate mixture. Turn into a serving dish, sprinkle with chopped nuts and serve immediately.

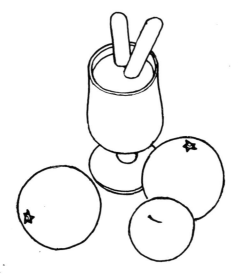

Flavoured Yogurt

1 pint (2½ cups) longlife
  (sterilized) milk
2 tablespoons plain yogurt
Flavourings:
1 tablespoon strawberry milk shake
  syrup
1 fresh strawberry to decorate

½ small bar peanut brittle, crushed
2 tablespoons chocolate milk shake
  syrup
1 oz. (1 square) plain (semisweet)
  chocolate, grated
1½ tablespoons liquid honey

Heat the milk in a sterilized saucepan until just warm—about blood
heat. Whisk in the yogurt and pour into 4 small sterilized dishes.
Cover with cling film (plastic wrap) and place in a large box or tin,
lined with cotton wool or paper. Cover and leave in a warm place
(an airing cupboard is ideal) for about 8 hours. Chill in the
refrigerator. When ready to serve, mix in any of the above
flavourings and decorate as shown.

The made yogurt should be kept unflavoured until ready for use,
and should keep for up to 1 week in a refrigerator.

To sterilize equipment before use, place in normal sterilizing
solution used for babies' bottles, etc.

Apricot Fool

2 oz. (⅓ cup) dried apricots
5 tablespoons water
few drops of lemon juice
2 teaspoons sugar

3 tablespoons double (heavy)
  cream, whipped
5 tablespoons plain yogurt
1 teaspoon slivered almonds, toasted

Soak the apricots in the water and lemon juice for at least 12 hours.
Simmer until tender, about 20 minutes. Sieve (strain) or purée the
fruit in a blender and sweeten to taste with the sugar.

Mix together the fruit purée, whipped cream and yogurt. Spoon
this mixture into a stemmed glass. Scatter flaked toasted almonds on
top. Chill in the refrigerator until set. Serve chilled.

Orange Meringue Pudding

1 orange
1 individual trifle sponge cake (slice
  of pound cake)
1 egg, separated

1 oz. (2 T) caster sugar
½ teaspoon cornflour (cornstarch)
¼ pint (⅔ cup) milk

Cut the orange in half. Grate the rind and extract the juice from one half; peel and slice the other. Cut the cake in half and place in a small ovenproof dish. Moisten the cake with the orange juice and arrange the orange slices on top. Beat the egg yolk with half the sugar and the cornflour (cornstarch). Heat the milk and orange rind and stir into the egg yolk mixture. Return to the pan and cook very gently, stirring until the custard thickens. Pour this over the oranges. Beat the egg white until stiff and gently fold in the remaining sugar. Pile onto the custard. Bake in a warm oven, 300°F, Gas Mark 2 for 20 minutes or place under a hot grill (broiler) until the meringue is brown. Serve hot.

Raspberry Omelette

2 eggs, separated
1 tablespoon single (light) cream
2 teaspoons caster sugar

½ oz. (1 T) butter
4 oz. (¾ cup) raspberries

Mix together the egg yolks, cream and sugar in a bowl. Beat the egg whites until stiff, then fold into the yolk mixture. Melt the butter in a 7 inch omelette pan. Pour in the egg mixture and let it cook gently on the underside. Place the omelette under a hot grill (broiler) still in the pan, to cook the top and allow the omelette to become puffy. Meanwhile, heat the raspberries in a saucepan until pulpy. Pour the raspberry pulp into the centre of the omelette, fold over once and slide it onto a warm plate. Serve immediately.

Apple Charlotte

1 oz. (2 T) butter, melted
1½ oz. (¾ cup) fresh breadcrumbs
1 oz. (2½ T) brown sugar
pinch of ground cinnamon

lemon juice
2 large cooking apples, peeled,
  cored and sliced
double (heavy) cream

Mix together the butter, breadcrumbs, sugar and cinnamon. Pour lemon juice over the bottom of a well-greased small ovenproof dish. Arrange the apples and breadcrumb mixture in layers in the dish, ending with a layer of the crumbs. Bake in a moderately hot oven, 375°F, Gas Mark 5, for about 30 minutes or until the apples are tender and the top is a golden brown. Serve hot with double (heavy) cream poured on top.

Dessert Banana

1 banana, sliced lengthways
½ oz. (1 T) butter
1 tablespoon brown sugar

2 tablespoons apple juice or cider
  (hard cider)

Carefully fry the banana in the butter in a frying pan (skillet). Place the slices in a warm serving dish. Melt the sugar in the butter remaining in the pan and gradually add the apple juice or cider. Cook for 1 minute, then pour over the banana. Serve hot.

Fruit Jelly with Cream

2 oz. (½ cup) redcurrants
2 oz. (½ cup) blackcurrants
2 oz. (½ cup) raspberries
2 teaspoons water
2 oz. (¼ cup) caster sugar
1 teaspoon arrowroot
2½ oz. (¼ cup plus 1 T) unsalted
  butter, cut up

1 oz. (2 T) caster sugar
2 oz. (½ cup) flour
½ oz. (2 T) cornflour (cornstarch)
few drops of vanilla essence
  (extract)
double (heavy) cream

Gently cook the fruits with the water until pulpy. Sieve (strain) the
fruits and dissolve the sugar in the purée, over a gentle heat. Dissolve
the arrowroot in a little water. Gradually add the purée and return
the mixture to the pan. Bring to the boil, stirring constantly. Pour
into a small glass dish and allow to set.

Meanwhile make the shortbread fans. Place all the remaining
ingredients, except the cream, in a bowl and work them together
with the tips of your fingers, until the mixture binds together.
Lightly knead the mixture, then roll out to a circle about ¼ inch
thick. Divide the circle into triangles and place on a greased baking
sheet. Bake in a moderate oven, 325°F, Gas Mark 3 for 15-20 minutes
or until light brown. Leave to cool slightly on the baking sheet
before transferring to a wire rack.

Keep most of the shortbread fans in an airtight biscuit (cookie) tin
for future use and serve two with the fruit jelly (gelatin). Pour cream
over the top of the jelly (gelatin) and serve immediately.

Ice Cream with Butterscotch Sauce

½ oz. (1 T) butter
1½ oz. (¼ cup) brown sugar
1 tablespoon milk

2 teaspoons honey
1 individual portion vanilla
  ice-cream

Put all the ingredients, except the ice-cream, in a saucepan. Cover the
pan and simmer gently for 20-30 minutes, until the sugar has
dissolved and the sauce is dark and thick. Pour the sauce over the
ice-cream, in a glass bowl, and serve immediately. This sauce is also
delicious with gingerbread or sponge cake.

FRUIT JELLY WITH CREAM
(Photograph: Danish Food Centre, London)

Stuffed Baked Orange

1 orange, peeled
2 dates, chopped
few almonds, chopped

1 tablespoon honey
2 teaspoons caster sugar
little lemon juice

Put the orange in a saucepan and cover with hot water. Simmer for 30 minutes. Drain the orange, reserving the liquid. Make a hole through the centre of the orange and place it in a small ovenproof dish. Stuff with the chopped dates and almonds. Boil together ¼ pint (⅔ cup) of the reserved liquid, the honey, sugar and lemon juice to taste for 2-3 minutes. Pour over the orange. Bake in a moderately hot oven, 375°F, Gas Mark 5 for 1 hour, basting with the syrup frequently. Cool and chill the orange before serving.

Alpine Orange

1 orange, peeled and segmented
½ oz. (1 T) caster sugar
2 teaspoons sherry
2 tablespoons double (heavy) cream

2 teaspoons milk
drop of vanilla essence (extract)
1 meringue, crushed

Put the orange segments and any juice in a bowl with the sugar and sherry. Chill thoroughly. Just before serving, whip together the cream and milk. Stir in the vanilla essence (extract) and crushed meringue. Pile this mixture on top of the orange segments and serve immediately.

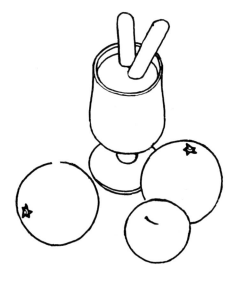

INDEX

INDEX